REMEMBER WHO YOU ARE

Chad Diamond Dann

The Pathfinder
The Journey of Becoming Yourself

Chad Diamond Dann

GRINDSTONE FILMS

Vancouver, Washington

This edition first published in December 2020
by Grindstone Films™, LLC

Subscribe to Chad's YouTube Channel by going to
www.youtube.com/chaddiamonddann
Instagram: @lionheartchad
Email: chaddiamonddann@gmail.com

ISBN: 978-0-578-78222-5

Cover Design by Hamar Artworks
Interior Design by Sarco Press
Edited by Madeleine Swart
Author Photo by Rachel Konsella Photography

Lyrics/Poems written by Chad Diamond Dann in Chapters 2, 3, 5 & 8
are from the album "Mr. Make It Happen." Copyright © Muzik Kaoz

GREATNESS IS MADE IN THE MUD

PLAY AROUND HAVE FUN!

This book is dedicated to everybody
That has ever felt the fire burn inside to be
Something extraordinary in this life.
If so, sign below.

My Name Is:

_____

I AM THE PATHFINDER

THE PATHFINDER

"I Promise"

I promise to show up with love and compassion
Live in the moment
Take inspired action

See, what's been missing is
We need to embrace our intuition
And make magic

I am completely aligned with the Divine
I promise

You can still be a man and not live in the program
You can't manifest if you ain't on the manifest
You can't die never not feelin' alive
One life, it can change in one night

I am, you can, I will be the light
I promise

- Chad Diamond Dann

Questions on Your Path

THE MOMENT OF SURRENDER IS NOT WHEN
LIFE IS OVER. IT'S WHEN IT BEGINS.

-Marianne Williamson

1.

Am I worthy enough to live my best life?

2.

Do I wholeheartedly trust myself?

3.

Why am I holding back my creativity and power?

Transformation Affirmations

UNLESS YOU LEARN TO FACE YOUR OWN SHADOWS,
YOU WILL CONTINUE TO SEE THEM IN OTHERS,
BECAUSE THE WORLD OUTSIDE YOU IS ONLY A
REFLECTION OF THE WORLD INSIDE YOU.

- Unknown

I created these affirmations to remind myself that I am a true light of hope and inspiration—that a cycle is ending and a new one begins full of harmony and freedom. My wish for you is that these affirmations will help you feel the same way. Salute!

For best results, say out loud and chant these affirmations as many times as you can in a row. Scream them at the top of your lungs, say them loud and proud with the people you love. Dance around, have fun. Feel the affirmations flowing through your entire body as you release them out into the universe!

1.

I AM ALIVE, I AM ENOUGH, I WILL CREATE

2.

IN THIS MOMENT
RIGHT HERE, RIGHT NOW, I AM WHOLE

3.

THE MAGIC, THE MYSTERY,
IT'S TIME TO MAKE HISTORY

CHAPTER ONE

DEAR CHAD

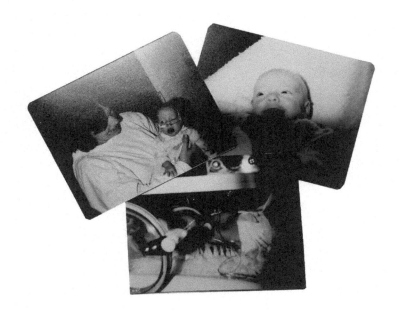

IF WE WANT TO DO SOMETHING GREAT,
ALL WE HAVE TO DO IS BE OURSELVES. IT'S THAT
SIMPLE.

- Dustin Anthony Coggi

*D*EAR *C*HAD,

You are an amazing, open-hearted, divine being. You are so powerful and worthy. Your voice will change lives, and your heart will change the world.

Chad, I am so in love with you. You are perfect in mind, body, and spirit. I will love you fiercely for the rest of your life. You are everything I ever wanted to be—imperfectly perfect, the way you were created. You deserve so much credit for everything you have accomplished in this life.

The best is yet to come. Be great, be yourself, and I will see you at the top.

Love,

Chad Michael Dann

P.S. I love you so much.

Love Yourself Ferociously

YOU BEING YOU IS A BLESSING.
YOU BEING YOU IS A MIRACLE.
YOU BEING YOU IS ENOUGH.
YOU BEING YOU IS YOUR SOUL SIGNATURE.

- Panache Desai

Man, I've spent a long time trying to find myself and truly discover who Chad is and how I can really love myself. I've had to work through so many doubts and worries and fears and the feeling that I'm not worthy, that I'm not good enough, the feeling that I've got to prove the world wrong—all that shit that's been programmed into our minds ever since we were kids.

The life experiences that I had knocked me down again and again. Through the good times and the bad times, this has been quite a journey. I've definitely learned always trying to gain others' approval, or striving to be a super successful person so that people will love me, see me, respect me, and welcome me with open arms, is incredibly exhausting.

I had to realize that it is truly all about the journey—about living, learning, growing, and moving forward no matter what comes my way. Understanding that baby steps equals greatness reps. Embracing the lesson that greatness is made in the mud, and that is how we rise. Asking myself hard questions, like: can I be grateful for what I have and let go of outcomes and expectations as I pursue my biggest dreams? That's something I've been working on my entire life, and it's been a hell of a ride.

So here I am, vulnerably writing my first book. I am an open heart. I am an open vessel. I am an open channel.

I am here to give you little pieces of my story, hoping to inspire you along your path. Just know that it's okay to be you and it's okay to still be finding yourself. It doesn't matter if you're 5 years old or 80 years old; I believe we never stop evolving, never stop growing, and that is a beautiful thing.

We are special because we are here, on this planet. What are the chances that this one little sperm went into this one little egg and you were born as a human being on a blue ball that's spinning in the middle of an infinite universe? The other day I was watching a TED Talk by Mel Robbins, and she said that scientists claim the chances are 1 in 400 trillion of being born a human being. Okay, Chad, I think we got something here.

I love thinking about it because I love the great mysteries of life. I love exploring and discovering more about myself in this crazy beautiful messy world.

I was born August 20th, 1981 at 6:42 p.m. in Cortland, New York. I came out two minutes after my fraternal twin brother Kurt because he had kicked me into my mom's ribcage. We were born two months early. One of my lungs was quarter-collapsed, and both my brother and I were under 4 pounds or so.

As the story goes, with my lung issues and being a preemie, I was in and out of the hospital for that first year of my life. My mom and dad told me how I would be at home with them and I would turn purple and stop breathing, and they would rush me to the hospital. Apparently I was read my last rites nine times. That means I was supposed to die *nine different times* within the first year of my life. I was a little miracle baby, if I do say so myself.

I kept fighting. I didn't give up, and now I live to tell my tale. Did I survive because I am supposed to be something great in this world? Was this the beginning of me feeling like I had to prove the world wrong, that I had to fight and claw my way through life to be accepted? Or was this destiny—destiny to truly find out who Chad really is in this human experience?

Maybe life is about being in the moment, following your joy, and being content with exactly who you are. Maybe, just maybe, by doing that you become aligned with your purpose, find your path, and fall completely in love with yourself.

When you look in the mirror, do you love everything you see and feel with your entire heart and soul? I'm not 100% there yet, actually. I have a long way to go. And if you're not there yet either, it's all good. I see you, my brothers and sisters. I love you for all that you are!

"Listen"

They all wanna know how I get so raw
7 months pregnant mama fell in the grocery store
Crying out her eyes couldn't take it no more
Screaming bloody murder trying to pray to the Lord

2 months early, hope my babies gonna live
She just found out that she about to have twins
She's got no insurance; she's got nothing to give
We was knocking at the door I think it's time to let us in

My brother came first I was stuck in her ribs
2 minutes later gave birth to the kid
But something went wrong, couldn't breathe, turned purple
Had the doctor and the nurse and the preacher in the circle

Please bless this baby 'cause he's done no wrong
Please give him strength so he makes it through the storm
Last rites read but I got to hold on
They looked at my face and seen the tears was gone

- Chad Diamond Dann

Questions on Your Path

LEARN FROM YESTERDAY, LIVE FOR TODAY,
HOPE FOR TOMORROW. THE IMPORTANT THING IS
NOT TO STOP QUESTIONING.

- Albert Einstein

1.

What makes me unique?

2.

What did I love to do as a kid that I don't do anymore?

3.

Do I love myself so ferociously it's almost dangerous?

Transformation Affirmations

THE GREATEST REVOLUTION IN OUR GENERATION IS THAT OF HUMAN BEINGS, WHO BY CHANGING THE INNER ATTITUDES OF THEIR MINDS CAN CHANGE THE OUTER ASPECTS OF THEIR LIVES.

- Marilyn Ferguson

I have created these affirmations for myself to empower me to step into a world of unlimited possibilities. My wish for you is that these affirmations will help you feel the same way. It is our birthright to live our best lives to infinity and beyond.

For best results, say out loud and chant these affirmations as many times as you can in a row. Scream them at the top of your lungs, say them loud and proud with the people you love. Dance around, have fun. Feel the affirmations flowing through your entire body as you release them out into the universe!

1.

MY GREATNESS AWAKENS MY PASSION & PATIENCE

2.

I WILL RISE, I AM UNBREAKABLE

3.

I AM A REFLECTION OF THE LOVE IN MY HEART

CHAPTER TWO

LISTEN TO YOUR HEART

ONLY DO WHAT YOUR HEART TELLS YOU.
- Princess Diana

I CAN REMEMBER THE time I started to try to be something I wasn't, to be something other than Chad so I would be accepted. It happened when I was probably 13 or 14 years old, riding on the school bus.

The kids on the school bus would always ruthlessly pick on me. They would pick on the way I looked. They would yell out to me, "Lazy eye, lazy eye!" (As I mentioned, I was born two months early, and in addition to fighting to stay alive with my lung issues, I was also born with a lazy eye.)

Their words hurt me because when they would scream that at me, I didn't feel normal. I didn't feel like I fit in. I didn't feel special at all.

I grew up in Upstate New York on the backroads. My parents did the best they could, and there was always food on the table, and I'm grateful for that—but we didn't have the latest Nikes and Starter Jackets, if you dig what I'm saying.

This was back in the '90s. Anyone who grew up in that decade might remember the song called "One of Us" by Joan Osborne. In that song, there's a lyric that goes, "*What if God was one of us? Just a slob like one of us?*" Those Top 10 radio stations were the shit back then, and it was a popular song, so it came on the radio a lot.

And whenever that song would come on, my bullies would start singing, "What if Chad was one of us?"—confirming that I wasn't one of them and I wasn't worthy. I felt like a piece of shit. It just tore me to pieces.

I remember going home and crying in my mom's arms one day. That's still a special moment for me because even though I could tell my mom felt helpless and she didn't know what to do, I can still remember and feel in my heart how loved and comforted I felt in that moment.

So what did I do? My friends and I started picking on the bullies that were picking on me. I was dishing it right back out to them.

I'll tell you right now, even though I was picking on them and laughing at them, it never felt right in my heart, but I kept doing it anyway.

I was finding Chad, but I wasn't doing it in an authentic way. I was trying to put a different version of me out there so that I would be accepted.

Who Are You Really?

NOBODY CAN TEACH ME WHO I AM.
YOU CAN DESCRIBE PARTS OF ME, BUT WHO
I AM AND WHAT I NEED IS SOMETHING
I HAVE TO FIND OUT FOR MYSELF.

- Chinua Achebe

As a kid, I always loved to perform. I loved to be silly. One year there was a play being put on at my high school for *The Hunchback of Notre Dame*. Even though I thought my friends would think I was stupid or geeky for trying out for the play, I decided to try out anyway. I read for a very small role, just a couple lines.

A day or two later, the English teacher told me she wanted to give me the leading role as Quasimodo, even though I didn't try out for that part. My initial reaction was, "What, are you saying I'm ugly? You saying I've got a hunchback?" I immediately turned down the role.

I regret that decision to this day. When you think about the movie or the play for *Hunchback of Notre Dame*, you realize Quasimodo was an outcast. He was scared to be himself and bullied by so many people. But after all he goes through, what happens? At the end of that story, he ends up stepping out of the darkness and into the light.

Quasimodo became the hero of the story, but I didn't know it back then. I didn't know that he broke free from his shackles and saved Esmerelda when she was being burned at the stake. By finding the courage within and facing his fears, Quasi tapped into exactly who he was born to be. Finally, he was embraced and loved by all for just being his true authentic self.

If I had just been myself, I would have accepted that role, and who knows what kind of ripple effect that would have created in my life?

In life, every decision we make in every moment leads us down a different path. I ask you this: If we truly listen to our hearts in every decision, will the path that we create be aligned with our destiny and the essence of who we are? There is only one way to find out!

"The World Needs a Hero"

Be yourself, take a leap of faith
If you need some help just look at your face
To the man in the mirror, that's you DON'T WAIT
To the woman in the mirror, you're beautiful CHASE

Don't wait for the gates this is HEAVEN ON EARTH
We all got a purpose, that's the reason for your birth
Start believing in your worth, your special work
Harder than you've ever gone, larger than you've ever known

POSSIBLE, look inside you UNSTOPPABLE
The world needs a hero, the people will follow you
Time to stand tall, stronger than a brick wall
Put your cape on when you hear the people call

- Chad Diamond Dann

Questions on Your Path

AND NOW HERE IS MY SECRET, A VERY SIMPLE
SECRET.
IT IS ONLY WITH THE HEART THAT ONE CAN SEE
RIGHTLY,
WHAT IS ESSENTIAL IS INVISIBLE
TO THE EYE.

- Antoine de Saint-Exupery

1.

How would I feel if I said YES to showing up as the real me?

2.

How would I feel if I said NO to things that don't feel right?

3.

What does my heart truly want in this moment?

Transformation Affirmations

BE YOURSELF, EVERYONE ELSE IS ALREADY TAKEN.

- Oscar Wilde

I created these affirmations for myself to step out into the world, brave and courageous. My wish for you is that these affirmations will help you feel the same way. As T.I. would say, "Big shit popping and little shit stopping."

For best results, say out loud and chant these affirmations as many times as you can in a row. Scream them at the top of your lungs, say them loud and proud with the people you love. Dance around, have fun. Feel the affirmations flowing through your entire body as you release them out into the universe!

1.

I CAN BE ANYONE, I CAN DO ANYTHING

2.

I AM THE WRITER OF MY DESTINY

3.

I AM A LEGEND; MY POWER IS I AM ME

CHAPTER THREE

THE STAR

WHEN I WEAR THE MASK,
I CAN BE SOMEONE DIFFERENT.
I CAN BE PERFECT ON THE OUTSIDE WHILE HIDING
THE REAL, FLAWED PERSON UNDERNEATH.

- Unknown

*G*ROWING UP AS a kid, into my teen years and throughout high school, I always felt like the outcast in my family.

I came from a family of truck drivers and mechanics, and all I wanted to do was sit in my room, listen to gangster rap music, and record my own radio shows on cassette tapes. Still to this day, I have never changed the oil or fixed anything on any of my cars by myself (lol). I started writing poems at a very young age, and I really connected to the lyrics and poetry of Hip Hop.

I was growing up on the backroads of New York in a trailer that was the same color as a Smurf with pieces of plywood covering holes in the floors. I was throwing up the westside sign, Walmart pants sagging to the floor, thinking I was a tough guy. I related more to the '90s East Coast vs. West Coast beef and the struggle of the up-and-coming rappers than I did to my own family.

Don't get me wrong, I had some great times growing up, and I am grateful for those memories—but sometimes at home, I didn't feel as special as the other kids. I didn't feel like I could make anything out of myself, period. In fact, I didn't think I would ever leave my hometown. I didn't get good grades in high school because I didn't care. I just wasn't studying or putting in any effort. I just wanted to be cool and accepted. To be honest, I turned into a little smart ass. I wasn't grateful for the things that I did have and the blessings that were already in my life.

I barely graduated high school, but I did it. Given my love of rap music and my passion for poetry, I decided that I was going to go for it. I was going to start writing and recording rap songs, and I wanted to be the number one rapper on the planet. That way, I would finally be respected and loved by all I came across.

So that's what I did. I started going to parties and freestyling off the top of my head. I started hanging out with new people that were really into rap music. I started writing songs. I created a character, a persona for myself. Chad Michael Dann became Diamond Ricelli.

Diamond Ricelli was my rap name, and it was the most confident version of myself. Diamond Ricelli's attitude was, "Fuck the world. I don't care who gets in my way, I'm going to be successful. I'm going to prove the world wrong." He was an unstoppable, carefree version of Chad. I ran with that persona, and guess what happened? Next thing you know, I felt like the man. Girls started giving me attention, I started getting respect from people, and my light was finally shining out into the world.

During my twenties, I was in straight up grind mode. I ended up releasing nine albums and performed shows on the East Coast and the West Coast. I was connecting with people. I was putting my music out on the internet and in the streets. I had a fan base.

The thing about my songs is there were a lot of songs I was writing from the heart, and that was the true me. True Chad was coming through. I was inspiring others. A lot of people showed me love over the years. Those moments meant everything to me. Then there were the songs I wrote because I was just trying to make hit records. Songs I wrote because I wanted to keep up with the latest waves, trends, and what other rappers were talking about. Some of those songs were super disrespectful towards women, and I am truly sorry about that today. I was working through so much trauma when it came to trusting women back then, and it showed.

I was talking the slick talk. I was talking a lot of shit about people in my lyrics. I called myself The Foul Mouth aka Mr. Fuck Your Sister at one point, along with many more crazy ass nicknames. I was living in this world I had created that felt really extreme and parts of it still felt wrong in my heart, just like picking on those kids back in high school.

Diamond was shining through, two-stepping his way to greatness, and Chad was more than happy to hop in the backseat most of the time. I was becoming something more. I finally felt like I existed in this world.

Grow Time!

I WANT TO GROW.
I WANT TO BE BETTER. YOU GROW.
WE ALL GROW. WE'RE MADE TO GROW.
YOU EITHER EVOLVE OR YOU DISAPPEAR.

- Tupac Shakur

In 2009, I was working as a cook at Cornell University, paying my bills and frustrated that I wasn't famous yet, so I decided to drop it all.

I had about $11,000 in my retirement fund. I took it out and headed out to California with 500 mixtapes in my suitcase. I decided I was going to Hollywood, baby. It was time to be discovered. My mixtape was called "Walking on Water," and I felt like I was walking on water, like I could do anything. I believed in myself so much.

I stayed with some friends and started grinding. I was walking down Hollywood Boulevard handing out CDs. I was in Huntington Beach with a boom box on the pier, rapping my new songs. I was doing livestreams before livestreams were even a thing.

One day, a successful businessman from Australia who had his own independent record label saw one of my livestreams. Next thing you know, I'm flying from LAX out to Australia and signing a record deal. The contract was for a one album deal with a lot of financial backing. I spent a month in Australia, writing new songs and honing my craft. Then we flew back to North Hollywood and recorded my album, Mr. Make It Happen, for the label. The experience was amazing. The songs were amazing.

I ended up flying back home to Upstate New York to visit for a couple weeks right after I recorded the album, just in time for my 30th birthday.

People came up to me on the streets of my hometown, asking for autographs. I thought I had made it. I thought I was about to be number one. My dreams had come true. I went into celebration mode. I was drinking mad alcohol, smoking weed, and popping pain pills like it was my day job. It seemed like a non-stop party for a hot minute. I was caught up in the hype and lost in the sauce.

I started pushing back when people from the label asked me to do things I didn't want to do. My ego was getting in the way in certain situations, and my deal fell apart before the album truly had the chance to be marketed. My relationships within the label suffered and just like that, the album was shelved for good.

Boom. In the blink of an eye, I'd gone from having a record deal and feeling like I made my dreams come true to losing it all. I officially moved back to New York with no job, no record deal, and an amazing album on the shelf. I was a failure. I was broken.

I always blamed the label for everything that happened, but I now understand the role my decisions and actions played in the fall of Diamond Ricelli with the Mr. Make It Happen album. I accept full responsibility, as I can clearly see I was finding my way. I have no regrets, though, because that part of my path contributed to the man I am today in a big way. During those times as Diamond, I took my biggest leaps and I danced with the unknown. I was becoming Chad.

"Valley of Death"

I feel like I walked a hundred thousand miles
I got no soles on my shoes
I got no soles on my shoes
THAT'S RIGHT

I feel like I walked a hundred thousand miles
Now tell me what you're gonna do
When the valley comes for you
TONIGHT

As I walk, walk, walk, walk, walk, walk
Through the valley of the shadow of death
The sky gets so clear and then the clouds reappear
THAT'S LIFE

As I walk, walk, walk, walk, walk, walk
Through the valley of the shadow of death
I know I am here and then I hear the crowd cheer
DIAMOND, DIAMOND, DIAMOND, DIAMOND

- Chad Diamond Dann

Questions on Your Path

EVERY ADVERSITY, EVERY FAILURE,
EVERY HEARTACHE CARRIES WITH IT
THE SEED OF AN EQUAL OR GREATER BENEFIT.

- Napoleon Hill

1.

Am I afraid to fail?

2.

What is the biggest risk I have taken so far in my life?

3.

What is my biggest, wildest dream that I
have not accomplished yet?

Transformation Affirmations

DON'T CHASE PEOPLE. BE YOURSELF, DO YOUR OWN THING AND WORK HARD. THE RIGHT PEOPLE— THE ONES WHO REALLY BELONG IN YOUR LIFE— WILL COME TO YOU. AND STAY.

- Will Smith

I created these affirmations for myself to show up with a heart the size of a lion. To seize the day my way. My wish for you is that these affirmations will help you feel the same way. Go out and get yours. I believe in you!

For best results, say out loud and chant these affirmations as many times as you can in a row. Scream them at the top of your lungs, say them loud and proud with the people you love. Dance around, have fun. Feel the affirmations flowing through your entire body as you release them out into the universe!

1.

I AM THE STAR OF MY OWN MOVIE

2.

I SHINE MY LIGHT, I AM UNDIMMABLE

3.

I CAN FLY, I HAVE FAITH WITH NO WINGS

CHAPTER FOUR

THE UNKNOWN

EVERY GREAT MOVE FORWARD IN YOUR
LIFE BEGINS WITH A LEAP OF FAITH,
A STEP INTO THE UNKNOWN.

- Brian Tracy

F I TOOK all my life experiences, put them in a pot and cooked up the most delicious Chad gumbo in the world, what do you think the main ingredient would be? Yes, my brothers and sisters, you are correct: that ingredient would be the unknown. A place not known or familiar. I am talking the big risk, FUCK THE PROGRAM, you cannot tell me how to live my life, leap of faith unknown. The type of risk where everyone around you thinks you have lost your mind for giving up any security and stability you may have had.

So before we get into what happened after I lost my record deal, I wanted to shine a little light on another story that impacted my life greatly in the realm of big leaps.

When I dropped everything and moved to California, it wasn't my first time stepping into the unknown. My first real time was in 2006, 7 years after I graduated from high school. I had released my first mixtape and was working on my second one (The Foul Mouth, Volumes 1 & 2). Those were the days of pressing CDs and selling them out of the trunk of your car type vibe.

At the time, I was making a lot of music with my friend Ave Mack from The Empire Kings and had a couple dope songs in the stash with my best friend Erik Mattox, aka Eklips (who later was the best man at my wedding, down the road).

Those were the Myspace days, and Ave made a connection on Myspace with a lady from the UK named Sonia, who ran a model agency and was connected in the music scene over there. She extended the offer for us to come over the pond to stay with her; she would help us get our music circulating overseas and we'd be able to do some shows. We were just young bucks in our mid-twenties, so we were like, "We're ready, man. We're ready to drop it all and go over to London."

I'm pretty sure Sonia even had it locked in for us to open up a show for Montell Jordan soon after we arrived, if I remember correctly.

Ave, his cousin Trey Skoolz, Eklips, and I decided to go to London. Four up-and-coming rappers truly trying to live out their dreams. I took a leave of absence from my job at Cornell University as a short order cook, sold my little hoopty rusty-ass car for about $130, moved out of my apartment, packed three suitcases (one of them was full of mixtapes), and left with $1,300 in my pocket. That was it. We trusted. We wanted to make it happen. It was the biggest risk that I had ever taken in my life up to that point.

Flying to London was my first time ever on a flight—7+ hours over the Atlantic Ocean. Finally, we got there and started going through customs at Heathrow Airport. As I recall, they had just stopped a terrorist attempt there a few weeks before, so there was definitely a heavy security vibe going on.

They went through our luggage and found CDs upon CDs. "You got a working visa to sell these?" they asked. "I'm just handing them out," I said.

It's hard to remember the details of the whole story, but I'm going to keep it simple. We were planning on staying with Sonia for somewhere between 3–6 months, and we had a lot of luggage. So, after a bunch of questions and tearing our luggage apart, customs red-flagged us and then we had to go deal with immigration.

Immigration put us in a holding cell for what seemed like 11 hours, feeding us cheese and pickle sandwiches. There were dudes on the ground praying, a couple of girls in the corner bawling their eyes out—it was intense energy. It was nuts.

They started questioning us one by one on why we were there. I tried to explain, "We're rappers. We're coming over here to push our music and we'll be staying with a friend."

The fact that I only had $1,300 in my pocket was def a concern for them. They wanted to know how I would survive staying that long without a job to make more money. And if I were going to be making money, I would need a working visa for that. To be honest, I can't remember everything that I was asked; all I remember is it felt like this intense interrogation.

Needless to say, immigration decided that they were not going to allow us into their country. Maybe all our stories didn't match up or we didn't have our paperwork right, or maybe it was the fact that we all only had one-way tickets there, but whatever it was, they were like, NOPE. They started working on getting us on the next available flight home to the States.

It turned out that Sonia had been waiting at the airport to pick us up the entire time and had been in contact with the immigration officers. Maybe they felt bad for all the shit they put us through, or maybe Sonia talked a good game, but eventually they came to us and said, "Give us your passports. We're going to let you go out into London for the night, but you have to be back tomorrow by 9 a.m. to be on a flight back home."

We jumped up and were ready to take on the night and whatever came our way.

I left my passport, packed like 150 mixtapes into my little book bag, and we went out and met with Sonia and her people. SMA, Kenny, Silvaa, what's good my brothers? We were drinking, freestyling, and just having a great time with our new friends.

We went out partying and handed out our music to as many people as we could. They were playing our tracks in the club, and it was an amazing feeling to see people from another country dancing to one of my songs.

We ended our night of drinking with some McDonald's. I've never seen a cleaner McDonald's in my entire life. The Big Mac I ate looked like it was straight out of a magazine. Everything from the soda bottles and outlets in the walls to the packs of cigarettes looked different to anything I was used to in America. It was def cool to experience a little taste of another country.

We headed back to the airport at around eight in the morning, still tipsy and feeling right. We got our passports back, grabbed our luggage, and headed to our gate. While we were waiting for our plane to arrive, we heard over the loudspeaker, "Erik Mattox and Chad Dann, will you please report to terminal blah blah blah."

We were a little blown away because we were in this huge airport with what seemed like thousands of people in it, and we were like, "They already shit all over our dreams; what do they want now?" At the same time, it almost felt like a divine sign or synchronicity that they would call our names specifically.

We got up to the customer service counter and found out that there were some issues with our seats on the plane to get us back. Apparently, the plane was totally full, and they had given up our seats to somebody else and wanted us to purchase tickets for another flight for later that day.

We told them, "Listen, you're sending us back. We're not paying extra. It's your decision to kick us out of this country, so get us on that plane."

They printed out new tickets for us, and we joined the others in time to board the flight. Ave and Tre found their seats first. Erik and I headed down the aisle looking for our spots.

When we got to our seats, there was a couple sitting in them. They checked their tickets and they were supposed to be in them. All we could really do at that point was laugh, like, "Wow, is this really happening?"

We went to tell the flight attendant, and she put us in one of those little side areas and said, "Here, have some champagne." So, we started chugging down multiple glasses, feeling like we were ballin'. Finally, she came back and said, "We found some seats for you guys. Follow me."

This was a huge plane because it was going from London to New York City. Think of the biggest plane you've ever seen—that was it. Erik and I followed the flight attendant, and we were getting closer and closer to the front of the plane. I said to Erik, "Yo, I'm pretty sure we're going into first class."

We got all the way to the front of the plane. There were three rows of huge first-class seats that leaned all the way back, with big screen

TVs—and this was 2006; I didn't even know they had these big screen TVs on planes.

We got up to seat 8A and she said, "Okay, Mr. Mattox, here's your seat." Erik sat down, smiling ear to ear, and gave me a dap. Then she said to me, "Mr. Dann, follow me." I swear to God, there was one extra beautiful first-class seat all by itself, and that was my seat. They put me in Seat 1A. I could literally see the pilot's back about 10 feet in front of me, and the only other thing in front of me was one side seat for the flight attendant to buckle in.

After risking it all—selling everything, leaving my apartment, leaving my job, partying in London for a night, basically getting deported back to the United States, and my seat being taken—I was now in Seat 1A, damn near close enough to fly the plane myself. If Jay-Z were on that flight, that would have been his seat. I felt like a king, and I know Erik did too.

I fully lay back, kicked my shoes off, and fell asleep before the plane even took off. I woke up over the Atlantic Ocean to a steak dinner and a hot steaming towel. The stewardess was a beautiful girl with an Irish accent. She gave me an oil arm massage. It was epic. I was getting treated like royalty. It was the craziest thing I could think of happening after everything we had gone through.

The Lesson

ALL JOURNEYS HAVE SECRET DESTINATIONS OF WHICH THE TRAVELER IS UNAWARE.

- Martin Buber

I absolutely knew in that moment with all my heart that something bigger than myself was happening. That there was a beautiful message in the lesson. That I was in perfect alignment and exactly where I was supposed to be. I was being rewarded for taking that leap into the unknown. God was saying, "Chad, keep walking your path, keep grinding. This timeline wasn't for you, but if you are true to yourself, this is what you can expect: abundance in all forms."

My fellow human beings, abundance is our birthright. Whatever that is for you, it is your choice. I'm not talking about just money, the greatest story ever told; I'm talking about showing up courageous and bold. Will you take a life-changing risk with me? Are you willing to lose it all, knowing you are simply unlocking the greatness within yourself? The unknown is where the magic is. It is where we get to meet the person we were born to be.

Repeat after me!

I AM A FORCE TO BE RECKONED WITH, SET ME FREE!

"The Unknown"

The Unknown
A place not known or familiar
A place where the great ones looked fear in the face
And screamed to the gods, "I will not go softly into that dark night"

It's time to be brave and courageous
Make 'em notice how ferocious you can be
When you embrace all that you are
The unknown, where the blind man sees

Take a look in the mirror and know
To discover your purpose, you got to believe that you're worth it
It's time to take a leap, have faith with no wings

You can fly, they can dream
You are, I believe, THE UNKNOWN

- Chad Diamond Dann

Questions on Your Path

TOO MANY OF US ARE NOT LIVING OUR DREAMS
BECAUSE WE ARE LIVING OUR FEARS.

- Les Brown

1.

How far have I come in the last 10 years?

2.

Am I a leader or a follower?

3.

If I faced my biggest fear, what would happen?

Transformation Affirmations

JUST WHEN THE CATERPILLAR THOUGHT THE WORLD WAS OVER, IT BECAME A BUTTERFLY.

- Chuang Tzu

I created these affirmations for myself to believe I am a one-of-a-kind superhuman being that deserves to live my best life. My wish for you is that these affirmations will help you feel the same way. Your time is now!

For best results, say out loud and chant these affirmations as many times as you can in a row. Scream them at the top of your lungs, say them loud and proud with the people you love. Dance around, have fun. Feel the affirmations flowing through your entire body as you release them out into the universe!

1.

I AM IN LOVE WITH THE UNKNOWN

2.

I AM TRANSFORMING INTO SOMETHING MAGNIFICENT

3.

I RELEASE ALL SCARCITY; I AM ABUNDANCE REBORN

CHAPTER FIVE

MAMA DON'T CRY

A BEAUTIFUL THING HAPPENED when I moved from California back to New York. Two days after the move, I was out having some drinks with my brother David Fairley, aka The Steel City Kid (one of my best friends and my hype man on stage for many years) at my friend Robby's spot, Brix Pubaria. I heard a female voice say to Robby, "Introduce me to him." I immediately looked over and locked eyes with Nealy Warfe.

It was such a familiar "Hey, there you are finally" type of look. An instant soulmate connection. Hiding my pain on the inside, feeling like my dreams had been crushed from the record deal situation, I was suddenly blessed with love at first sight to help heal my wounds. I moved in with Nealy about 3 weeks later and we have been together ever since. I realized the lesson was a blessing in disguise and kept pushing forward. I love you schmooey!

I was still making new music, I was still doing shows, but I also wanted to try some new things.

I decided I was going to learn how to film and edit my own music videos because honestly, I was broke and couldn't afford to pay somebody to do it for me. So, I bought my first camera and started going hard with the YouTube tutorials. I started shooting some videos for other local musicians as well and really developed a passion for filmmaking.

It was August 28th, 2012, a little over 8 months into Nealy's and my relationship, when I experienced the most difficult day of my life. I'd just finished shooting a music video for a dude named Ernest Verb in Ithaca, New York, and I was in the editing phase. Nealy and I were over at our friend's house. I had my laptop and was editing the video at the kitchen table, and everyone else was just visiting and chilling.

Then Nealy came up to me and said, "I think I'm going to go over and visit your mom for a few minutes." My mother and father lived about 15 minutes away.

For some reason, I got pissed suddenly. I was like, "What do you mean, you're going to visit my mom? *I* want to go visit my mom." There was this weird feeling inside that I had to go over to her house.

Nealy said, "You can just stay here and keep working on your video if you want," but I told her, "No, I've got to go."

We stayed and visited with my mom throughout that day, and I continued to work on the music video while we were there. Something seemed a little off with her. The doctors had her on all types of medication—depression medicine, bipolar medicine, painkillers, muscle relaxers. Pretty much you name it, she was on it, due to her lifetime full of crazy amounts of trauma that I will not even get into in this book.

She just had that look in her eyes. You know when you're looking at somebody and they're looking at you, but they're almost looking through you and their eyes are glazed over, kind of like they're not even in their body? That's what she looked like. I asked her, "Mom, what's wrong?" She said the doctor had just put her on a new medication about three days before. Another muscle relaxer or something. She said ever since she'd started adding it in with her other medications, she couldn't get out of her own way.

My mom trusted that whatever the doctor had her on was what she needed to be on. Why would a doctor do anything other than give patients what they need to be healed, right?

Later on that night, my mom was sitting in her recliner that was connected to the couch, watching TV, half falling asleep. That's where she slept most nights because of her bad back, and she had to constantly get up to go to the bathroom.

I had just finished up editing. I went over to her and showed her the music video. I then lay down on the couch next to her and snuggled up with her like I did as a kid.

She got up to go smoke a cigarette on the front porch, so Nealy and I went outside with her and decided to head home for the night.

She asked us if we wanted to go camping with her that coming weekend because she wanted to get out of the house. She wanted to do something she loved, and she loved going camping and sitting around the fire.

We said, "Yeah, we'll go camping with you." I gave her a huge hug and a kiss goodbye and told her how much I loved her.

She said, "I love you, too. I love you so much, sweetheart."

Nealy and I went back to our apartment and I fell asleep on the couch.

Dark Night of the Soul

THE JOURNEY OF THE DARK NIGHT OF THE SOUL IS WHERE WE LEARN WHO WE ARE, WITHOUT PEOPLE TELLING US.

- Adele Green

I suddenly woke up to a phone call. It was my sister, Abby. I was like, "Why is Abby calling me at four in the morning?" I almost didn't answer it. Then I thought maybe something was wrong.

I answered. "Hello?" My eyes were barely open.

"Chad?" Abby's voice was shaking. I could hear and feel the sadness in her whole being. "Mom's dead."

"What are you talking about, Mom's dead? I just saw her. I just left the house at 9:00. She was okay."

She said, "Dad just found her on the bathroom floor. Mom's dead." Abby was bawling her eyes out, and I felt like my heart was about to explode. I did not want to believe it; I could not accept it.

I can't remember exactly what happened next. All I know is the phone hung up and I started crying and ran into the bedroom, where Nealy was. I shook her awake and tried to tell her. She was like, "What? What?"

I said, "Mom's dead." I dropped to my knees, collapsed on the bed.

I've never cried so fucking hard in my life. Every inch of my soul and every molecule in my entire body was in pain, was screaming, was hurting.

Nealy and I rushed over to my mom's house. We were the first ones there besides my Aunt April. We got out of the car, and I was still crying my eyes out, barely able to catch my breath.

My dad, my hardworking father, the man's man, the grinder, not really known for his emotions—not that I'd seen much of growing up, at least—was on the porch, and he looked up at me with tears in his eyes and said, "Chad, Mom is gone."

It was the most horrible feeling, the most pain I've ever felt in my entire life. She was in there, lying on the bathroom floor. She'd woken up in the middle of the night to go to the bathroom, and then we're not really sure what happened, but she stopped breathing. I believe it was from the mixture of pills that doctor had her on, but the autopsy came up with no results on the cause of death.

If you had looked at my mom's cellphone contacts, you would have seen that she had me in her phone as "Chad, my little sweetheart." I was special to her. I was the only kid in the family who wasn't named after somebody else in our family lineage, and no matter how much I pushed her buttons growing up, I know deep down she always believed in me.

My mom's name was Kim Marie Dann. She was 52 years old. I love you and miss you every day, Mama.

I went into a year-and-a-half-long depression. I was still recording some music and doing shows, but I couldn't really get my mojo back, in my opinion. I was sick of doing the same old thing. I wasn't creating as much as I wanted to. I wasn't really looking for work. I had moments of inspiration and motivation during this time, but I was lost.

We needed some money coming into the house. Nealy was paying for and taking care of everything. So, I got a job at Subway for like $8.50 an hour. I'd gone from having a record deal to my mother dying to working at Subway. I felt like a piece of shit. My pride was hurt, my ego was hurt, but I did it and humbled myself quickly.

Eventually I was promoted to manager, making $9 an hour. One day, I was training a new girl and I told her, "I'm going to go out for a break. I'm going to smoke a cigarette." (That's when I still smoked cigarettes.)

But throughout that day, I kept getting these visions. I kept seeing my mom in my head and hearing her voice.

One thing I didn't tell you is when I was sitting on that couch the night she died and showing her my music video, she looked at me and said, "Sweetheart, I think you've got something here. I think you should pursue this. You're really good at this." Those words kept repeating over and over in my head as I saw my mom's face.

I told the new trainee I'd be back. But I never came back. I took off my apron, walked out of Subway, hopped in my car, and took off. I decided right there in that moment, at 33 years old, I was going to film school.

My darkest nights have led me to find the strength to shine my brightest light. Thank you, Mama. I now know LOVE can give a blind man sight. Greatness is made in the mud, play around have fun, LIVE LIFE! I know you are with me.

"Mama Don't Cry"

I know you feeling all alone
Now your kids grown up and they barely coming home
Dad still on the road and he still working hard
And you still in the trailer park wishing on a STAR, MAMA

Your son going far, Mama
I pray every day that you have no drama
Where your life and every single moment is perfect
Where you feel like everything you did was worth it

Keep your eyes on the prize, keep the truth in your heart
Just forget about the lies you were told when you were young
You can do anything, I'm a product of you, Mama
CAN YOU HEAR THE ANGELS SING?

Mama don't cry, no more tears
No more doubts, no worries, no fears
No more pain, I know you paid the cost
Think about your kids on those days that you're lost

Mama don't cry, no more tears
No more doubts, no worries, no fears
No more pain, I know you paid the cost
Think about your kids on those days that you're lost

Mama don't cry (cry, cry)
Mama don't cry (cry, cry)
MAMA DON'T

- Chad Diamond Dann

Questions on Your Path

UNABLE ARE THE LOVED TO DIE, FOR LOVE IS IMMORTALITY.

- Emily Dickinson

1.

Am I grateful for the gift of life?

2.

Can I see this moment for what it truly is?

3.

If time did not exist, who would I BE?

Transformation Affirmations

TRANSFORMED PEOPLE
TRANSFORM PEOPLE.

- Richard Rohr

I created these affirmations for myself, for when I fall and then I hear the call of the wild, I will rise from the ashes like the phoenix. My wish for you is that these affirmations will help you feel the same way. Spread your wings and fly, Young Phoenix!

For best results, say out loud and chant these affirmations as many times as you can in a row. Scream them at the top of your lungs, say them loud and proud with the people you love. Dance around, have fun. Feel the affirmations flowing through your entire body as you release them out into the universe!

1.

MY VOICE WILL CHANGE LIVES

2.

MY HEART WILL CHANGE THE WORLD

3.

I AM SO THANKFUL FOR ALL THAT I HAVE

CHAPTER SIX

THE PHOENIX

SOMETIMES YOU JUST HAVE TO
DIE A LITTLE INSIDE
IN ORDER TO BE REBORN AND RISE AGAIN
AS A STRONGER AND WISER VERSION OF YOU.

- Aagam Shah

I STARTED COLLEGE IN September 2014 to get my degree in Digital Cinema.

I've got to tell you, I was really nervous at first. I walked into the new student orientation with my camouflage shorts on, rocking a bandana like I was straight out of the *Sons of Anarchy* TV show. I was surrounded by all these 18-year-olds, and needless to say I didn't feel like I fit in right out of the gate.

Over the last 14 years, all I ever really wanted to be was a famous rapper, and other than my sister and my mother, not many people had called me "Chad" in years. It was always either Diamond or Dime.

College is when I finally started to be comfortable being called "Chad" again, and to be comfortable with people getting to know Chad. I was way outside of my comfort zone. I had been out of high school for a long time, so I had to learn how to retrain my brain and let information come in. I had to learn how to build a routine again, how to focus on my new goals.

And that's what I did for the next 2 years straight: go to my college classes, come home, do my work, sleep, and repeat. For 2 years straight I focused on nothing but my studies. In high school I didn't give a shit and I got horrible grades, but I really took this seriously because I wanted to come out of that 2-year program and start my own business. I had my eyes on the prize and I was believing in myself again.

I learned about the Hero's Journey in storytelling and realized that I was on my own Hero's Journey. I was the star of my own movie.

I ended up doing amazingly well in college. I graduated with a 3.8 GPA. One semester I even got a 4.0. Can you believe that? A 4.0. I made some dope short films, did an internship in Silicon Valley, and made some amazing new friends.

It felt good to just be me and shine my light during my college days. I was discovering new talents, pushing myself to grow, and remembering how smart I really was. I felt worthy.

I also created my first documentary, *One Love: The Eric Tallman Story*. I submitted the film to a New York statewide college film festival, and I was the first person from our school ever to be accepted into that festival.

I came out of college as an award-winning documentary filmmaker, taking home the Audience Choice Award. I'm grateful for the support that my community at Tompkins Cortland College gave me. They all believed in me.

I had risen from the ashes like the phoenix on this new path. I was all in. I was finding pieces to the Chad puzzle I didn't even realize I had lost.

The Fool & the Hanged Man

IF THE PATH BEFORE YOU IS CLEAR, YOU'RE PROBABLY ON SOMEONE ELSE'S.

- Joseph Campbell

I graduated in springtime 2016. Nealy and I got married that July, and I officially started my own business, Grindstone Films. At first I wasn't making a ton of money, but I was making enough to help pay the bills, and it was my full-time job. I was running my own business and doing a hell of a job at it.

I loved capturing the essence of people in the moment and weaving together the footage like a magician when editing it. I got on the grind and started making a name for myself. Some videos I did for local businesses and community events were getting thousands and thousands of views.

I even ended up shooting and editing a video that helped win my city a $10 million grant from the state of New York. Shout out to the amazing team I worked with on that project.

Then, in late August 2017, I got a call from a friend who lived in Vancouver, Washington, all the way on the West Coast (I had actually lived with him and his family in California years before). He asked me, "What is it going to take for me to get you out here to be the creative director for my company? I see what you're doing back in New York, and you're inspiring me. I want to hire you."

I tossed a ridiculous number at him and he said yes. I signed a 1-year contract and next thing you know, Nealy and I and our two cats were moving to the West Coast. We arrived on January 4th, 2018.

I met a lot of amazing people working for his company that year—speakers, coaches, healers, artists—and I shined my magic out into the world. I honed my craft and really built up my skill set, especially with shooting, editing, client interaction, and collaborating with others. But even though my title for the company was Creative Director, I felt limited in making any creative decisions. I was making a shit ton of money and felt stable and secure, though, so I just put my head down and did the work that needed to be done.

I lost 50 pounds on a weight loss program during that year and went through a spiritual awakening. I was accessing that place where I was living in the moment, and I really wanted to follow my joy. I started doing some motivational speaking and dropping life gems on my social media accounts as I was going through this new transformation. I had forgotten how much I loved talking my talk. I had focused so long on being behind the camera, telling other people's stories; I wanted to be back in front of it, telling mine. I wanted to get back to creating my vision on my terms, and working for someone else was simply not for me. I was being called by my higher self (the dopest version of Chad you can fathom) to change directions on my path.

So, after my 1-year contract was up, I went solo again with Grindstone Films on January 1st, 2019, ready to stake my claim on the West Coast. My first year in business, I made millions, got the white picket fence, had a batch of kids, and I lived happy ever after in the matrix like a good little human. NOPE!

I got to keep it real with y'all. 2019 on my own as a business owner in a still brand-new city was exhausting mentally, physically, and spiritually. I was fighting my shadow every step of the way, growing through drama and old traumas coming to the surface constantly. I was building my business, but behind the scenes I was lost in a scarcity mindset. I was no longer stable and secure in my mind, and I felt the weight of the world on my shoulders to be responsible for all our finances.

I had to take whatever job came my way because the bills needed to get paid and it was my job to grind my ass off. I didn't know how to say NO. I had no boundaries. I didn't trust that I could have flow and ease in my business.

This life-changing year wasn't all doom and gloom, though, my friends. I did do the inner work as it came up and grew tremendously. I did have some clients that I absolutely loved and created some amazing content for. I started a YouTube page and started filming some episodes of my own web series called "Good Morning to Greatness." I released some Spoken Word videos.

I loved those moments, but I was experiencing a lot more doubt than joy in my life. I put other people's happiness over mine. I was giving way more than I was receiving. I was living in fear. I was back in the mud, and I had put myself there by not being grateful for what I already had. I truly forgot how far I had come in life up to that point. I was BEYOND burnt out.

I was missing all the other pieces of me—the artist, the poet, the person who wants to just BE without worrying about paying taxes.

After my mother's death I rose from the ashes. I was born again and forged a brand-new path. I accomplished my goals and stepped into moments of my greatness. But now, once again, I am hearing a calling for something different. Do you hear the call of the wild? The call from your highest self? The call to remember who the fuck you are?

It is time we fly in a different direction, a direction that requires us to truly surrender to what is meant for us. A path that feels so right it cannot be wrong. A path of intuition over money. A path of flow and ease, yes, give me more please. No scarcity, no doubts, no worries, no fears. We will rise again; we are the Phoenix!

Let us use our stories to find the strength inside to let go of everything that has ever held us back. Are you ready to live your life the best way, aka your way? Are you ready to believe we live in a world of unlimited possibilities? Are you ready to fully TRUST and RECEIVE the abundance that is your birthright?

I know you are, and I am too. That is why I am writing this book. I cannot be the only one that feels this way. How are we going to show up in the world from this moment forward?

OUR TIME IS NOW!

"The Phoenix"

Let me ask you a question
Are you ready to rise up from the ashes, young phoenix?
Greatness is made in the mud, play around have fun
That's GENIUS

This is the moment we've been waiting for
Quarantined in boxes with doors
The rebirth of the NEW EARTH, Ascension is yours
A blessing of course, RISE UP

Time's up, or does it exist
In a different timeline where the poor are the rich
Unshackle our wrists
RISE UP, YOUNG PHOENIX

- Chad Diamond Dann

Questions on Your Path

IF THE PATH BE BEAUTIFUL, LET US NOT ASK WHERE IT LEADS.

- Anatole France

1.

In which areas in my life do I need to set better boundaries?

2.

Am I a people pleaser? Can I say NO?

3.

Am I a magnet for everything that I desire?
Can I trust I will receive everything I require?

Transformation Affirmations

YOUR INNER FIRE IS YOUR PASSION AND CREATIVITY.
IT'S YOUR LIFE FORCE ENERGY.

- HeatherAsh Amara

I created these affirmations to remind myself that I am loved and there will never be another me. I am a skyscraper of untapped potential. My wish for you is that these affirmations will help you feel the same way. Release and find peace.

For best results, say out loud and chant these affirmations as many times as you can in a row. Scream them at the top of your lungs, say them loud and proud with the people you love. Dance around, have fun. Feel the affirmations flowing through your entire body as you release them out into the universe!

1.

I'M IN LOVE WITH MY SHADOW

2.

I AM ETERNAL BEAUTY

3.

I RELEASE ALL THAT DOESN'T SERVE ME
I SWERVE ON THE HATERS

CHAPTER SEVEN

3 ANGELS

IN EVERY MOMENT, THE UNIVERSE IS WHISPERING
TO YOU. YOU'RE CONSTANTLY SURROUNDED BY
SIGNS, COINCIDENCES, AND SYNCHRONICITIES,
ALL AIMED AT PROPELLING YOU IN THE DIRECTION
OF YOUR DESTINY.

- Denise Linn

S O HERE I am, writing this book during the coronavirus pandemic in the year 2020. I've had the chance to finally get some flow and ease.

I remember about two weeks into the shutdown, I was out in nature meditating. I was at complete peace and I heard this voice in my head say, "Enjoy, this is what you have been waiting for." With all the chaos, uncertainty, and fear in the world, I had no option but to fully trust and surrender to the flow of life. I knew "every little thing's gonna be all right," just like Bob Marley said.

During the pandemic I have started living more in the moment. I am following my joy and working on things that excite me, but at the same time I am processing and purging old belief systems and patterns, and my deepest wounds have come to the surface. I've started seeing sign after sign, synchronicity after synchronicity that I am headed in the right direction and I am in alignment with who I was born to be.

In the beginning of June 2020, I got a phone call from my friend CoCo Leary, who I hadn't talked to in months. She's an amazing speaker, author, and inspiration to many people. I know CoCo came from the bottom, from the other side of the tracks, and I can relate to that. People like us have a unique quality called IT. That is something that cannot be taught.

As soon as I got on the phone with CoCo, she asked me how I was doing. Part of me thought, "Oh, I've got to tell her that I've been learning all of these new skills and my business is taking off in a new direction," but I couldn't. I had to keep it real because that's who I am. I started spilling my guts. I told her that I'm in the process of finding a new path again and I want to create and work on more content for myself so I can truly shine my light. I just wasn't exactly sure what that looked like yet. To be honest, I didn't have much clarity at that time; I was a little lost and was working through the feelings of being okay with that.

CoCo said, "Chad, I think it's time for you to write a book. It's time for you to use your voice. Your own book is the new business card."

I realized in that moment that my life *is* my message. By giving the world all of me in this book, I could help others find their way as I find mine, and if it reaches only one person, and that person finds the strength to be unapologetically, extraordinarily them, then job well done.

I believe the call with CoCo was in divine timing, a divine message that it was time to get started on creating the reality I truly want to live. In some way I feel the jumpstart she gave me that day was a reminder to herself of the greatness within her. Thank you, CoCo, so much for the inspiration. I truly appreciate you.

The Message

TO FIND YOUR ANGELS, START TRUSTING YOUR INNER VOICE AND INTUITION.

- Melanie Beckler

So, I started writing. I listened to my heart and the words started flowing. Some mornings I would get up and go to the park near my house, lay out a blanket, and lie there in the sunshine, feeling the earth underneath me, and write in complete peace. With no expectations around the outcome or where it would take me, I just wrote.

I want to talk about three angels I encountered on one of those days. You might think it sounds crazy, but I'm going to keep it one hundred with you and tell you the story anyway.

Angel #1

On June 26th, 2020, I was feeling down in the dumps that morning. I wanted to get some writing done, hug a couple trees, roll around in the grass, shit like that. I say the weirder the self-care, the better (lol).

As I walked through the park, I had a pillow in my left hand, a blanket in my right hand, and my backpack with all my writing supplies in it on my back. I was walking to the farthest corner of the park, towards some big trees where there's a beautiful pond. A gentleman was at the pond that day, fishing. He was just starting to pack up his fishing gear as I walked by.

He looked at me and smiled. I kept walking, and he asked, "Oh, you've got a blanket there?" I looked back at him and said, "Yeah."

In that moment I felt this pull from my chest to his, almost like there was a burst of white light connecting us. The energy was crazy. I turned around to keep walking, and he yelled out, "Yo, bro, you want a beer?" I turned around and thought, *I don't even really drink beer, but why not?*

So, I went back. I trusted the message I was getting, and I received the gift. I mean, who is going to turn down a beer from an angel? I took the beer from the man, put it in my backpack, and walked away.

The message I received from Angel #1 was to embrace the moment I was living in, to be grateful for all the beauty around me, and to not forget to have some fun. Chad, kick back and have a beer, bro. Enjoy the little things. A weight was instantly lifted from my heart and my heavy morning turned into a glorious day; I was walking on a cloud.

Angel #2

Later that day, I went back to my apartment and a couple of friends came over. We went outside and we were chilling on the grass, having a good time, talking about life and pulling some Oracle cards.

All of a sudden, I looked up and boom, there's Angel #2. It was an older lady with gray hair, riding by on a bicycle. As soon as our eyes met, once again, I felt this instant connection. It looked like she had a white aura around her as she was riding by.

She yelled out, "I hope you guys are having an amazing day! Enjoy it."

Message #2: You are exactly where you need to be. Every decision that you've ever made has led you to this exact point where you can be in the moment and enjoy the flow. Don't worry about what tomorrow brings.

Angel #3

A couple hours later, my wife and I and our friend Elizabeth decided to go for a walk. We walked to Target, which was a half a mile down the road. I decided to go barefoot because it's literally one of my favorite things ever.

They went into Target and I sat outside and waited for them (obviously, I couldn't go in because I didn't have any shoes on). It was the perfect weather—probably 78° with the most beautiful breeze and clear skies. Not too hot, not too cold. Just perfect. As I sat there on the bench, up pulled Angel #3 in an SUV.

She got out and started walking towards the entrance. When she got closer, she stopped and turned to me, and even though she had a mask on, I could tell she had the biggest smile on her face. She said, "Hi, how are you?"

Boom, as soon as she said it, I saw the light. That connection and energy pull between us was intense.

She said to me, "You look so peaceful on that bench. Are you enjoying the weather?"

I answered, "Yeah, I decided to walk over here with bare feet because I like feeling the earth on my feet."

She said, "Yes, feeling your feet on the earth is so good for your spirit."

"It's such a beautiful day," I said.

She replied, "Yes, what a blessing from God. This is the perfect day. If I didn't have to go in here, I would come right over there and be sitting with you and enjoying this moment with you."

I smiled so big and told her to have an amazing night and she walked inside. At this point my body was straight chills as I knew she was Angel #3. The message was clear. Be yourself, be here now and all will be revealed. We do not have to walk our paths alone.

All these signs and synchronicities, all the reflections and the work I've been doing during the quarantine, everything is leading me to be able to fully embody the real me—that baby who was born two months early with a superhero cape on, ready to fly. Little Chad who believed in a world of unlimited possibilities before he was told "you are never going to make anything out of your life."

We don't have to live by the blueprint of society. We can be happy if we don't have a shit ton of money. We can be happy if we don't have dope cars and a beach house in Cali. We can be happy by just creating what we were meant to create and trusting it will be what it is meant to be. I believe the creator created us to create things using the unique gifts that we all have. I am an artist; we are all artists.

Are you hearing the call to truly be the writer of your destiny? If you are not, THIS IS YOUR SIGN! This is your King/Queen Kong moment to beat on your chest and scream, "Here I am."

"Keep Growing"

Baby steps equals greatness reps
You get disappointed quick if you chase the checks
In the Matrix YES, you can be NEO
Talk your talk, you're the voice of the people

Show me a door that we can't kick down
You're a King, you're a Queen, you were made for the crown
Right here, RIGHT NOW, in the moment
We grow, we know how to OWN IT

Open up your eyes, I am I
We were born with a fire inside
LIGHT IT UP, it's time we arrived
The truth is the lesson is a BLESSING IN DISGUISE

- Chad Diamond Dann

Questions on Your Path

THE MOST IMPORTANT QUESTIONS IN LIFE CAN NEVER BE ANSWERED BY ANYONE EXCEPT ONESELF.

- John Fowles

1.

Is it possible for me to just BE?
(No matter how much chaos is going on in the world)

2.

When was the last time I went outside to play?
(Like I did as a little kid)

3.

What is my deepest wound and how can I heal it?

Transformation Affirmations

IN THIS MOMENT, THERE IS PLENTY OF TIME.
IN THIS MOMENT, YOU ARE PRECISELY AS YOU
SHOULD BE.
IN THIS MOMENT, THERE IS INFINITE POSSIBILITY.

- Victoria Moran

I created these affirmations to remind myself that I came out of the womb on a mission to make you listen, that my magic is mine and I will use my gifts to weave and receive, believe, and retrieve my blessings indeed. My wish for you is that these affirmations will help you feel the same way. You are a legend!

For best results, say out loud and chant these affirmations as many times as you can in a row. Scream them at the top of your lungs, say them loud and proud with the people you love. Dance around, have fun. Feel the affirmations flowing through your entire body as you release them out into the universe!

1.

I RELEASE, I FLOW, I BELIEVE, I KNOW

2.

I EMBRACE THE REALMS OF THE EXTRAORDINARY

3.

GOOD VIBRATIONS, NO LIMITATIONS

CHAPTER EIGHT

HERE I AM

I AM ALWAYS STRIVING TO HAVE A MORE CREAMY
DREAMY LIFE, IN EVERY WHICH WAY,
AND TO ALSO PROVIDE THAT
FOR THE PEOPLE THAT I LOVE.

- Jennifer Dadigan

ERE I AM, writing this last chapter and 2020 is almost over. The world is in chaos, but I believe a beautiful transformation is taking place to create a world we all love living in. The veil has been lifted, and people are waking up to their truth and potential.

Raise your hand if you went deep within during 2020. Raise your hand if you had childhood trauma come to the surface to be released. Raise your hand if you felt depressed and did not want to get out of bed. Raise your hand if you lost the passion for your business or you just didn't want to go back to your 9-to-5 job that drained your soul. Raise your hand.

I feel you, and I am right there in the mud with you. That is why I am sharing my stories and spilling my guts to you, because I am waking up to something greater inside of myself: an old friend named Chad ready to start a new chapter in life.

I am the phoenix in action. I am literally a work of art. We are all works of art. I know and believe we are all transmuting into something magnificent.

I am on that part of my journey. I am literally on my Julia Roberts *Eat, Pray, Love* shit right now. I'm totally okay with being in the moment and not putting myself in a box, not putting labels or titles on who I am or what I need to do, and trusting that I can follow what my intuition says, follow my heart, do what excites me, and know that I'm going to be okay.

That's what we were born to do.

One day I was on a Zoom call with my good friend and master hypnotist Mary Lou Rodriguez. She was working on a project to show people how they can create their reality, so needless to say the vibes were super high on the call.

As we talked, I was in the moment, and the words were flowing out of me when she stopped me. "Wait, what did you just say?" She wrote down what I said and read the quote back to me. It was something I hadn't even realized I said.

I said: *The lifeforce of our spirit is the art that we create.*

We are all artists. We are all unique. We are all given our own paintbrush with which to paint. But we've been programmed and brainwashed our entire life to live a certain way. How unique and special and magnificent we are to be created and put on this earth! And yet most of us do not even realize how amazing we truly are.

As the Pathfinder, we never stop growing. We never stop evolving, but we must learn to trust our inner radar. We were not born to just work our asses off, pay bills, and then die. This radar of unlimited potential speaks to us. It lives outside of a scarcity mindset. It lives outside of what other people think about us. It lives outside of the box so many people are afraid to step out of.

That radar is the highest version of ourselves talking to us, and it's saying, "Follow me. Follow me down this path. Follow me into the unknown where the greatest human beings that ever existed once played."

I am not an expert at life. I am not a life coach. This book is not here to teach you how to find your path. I'm telling my story, and maybe you need to hear it—but most importantly, I'm writing this book because I need to hear this too.

This is what I'm going through right now. I am awakening. I need this to be inspired, to keep taking steps, to keep following my intuition and become who I was meant to be.

The Oath

INTEGRITY IS THE MOST VALUABLE AND RESPECTED QUALITY OF LEADERSHIP. ALWAYS KEEP YOUR WORD.

- Brian Tracy

So, I am claiming right now, here I am.

My name is Chad and I have a heart the size of a lion. It is time for the world to hear me roar. Will you join me?

(If you feel the calling, please repeat after me)

I am going to only do what feels good and what feels right.

I am going to live in the moment, love, and play like a kid on his birthday.

I am going to trust I can fully show up as me and create my reality.

I am going to reach for the stars and enjoy the little things like bare feet in the grass and drinking water from mason jars.

I am going to live a life of flow and ease and be thankful for the blessings I receive.

I am going to use my gifts to inspire and lift humanity as it shifts.

And of course, when my shadow comes out to play, I will own it and do the work.

I have no idea what this book is going to do, and that's the beautiful thing. I'm writing this book with no expectations. Maybe I'll only publish 10 copies, and maybe you're 1 of the 10 people that got this book and you're reading it right now. Maybe it inspires you in this moment to walk your true path. Maybe it inspires you to do what you want to do and not what everyone else wants you to do. Maybe right here, right now you decide to live life on your terms.

So, I ask you: Are you ready to be in the flow? Are you ready to create from a place of excitement? Are you ready to smile and laugh and play like a child again? Are you ready to be your true self without worrying about what other people think? Are you ready to step out into the world and be a light that shines so bright, you can light up Tokyo?

Ladies and gentlemen, I'm asking you this because I'm asking myself that same question in this current moment.

My answer: YES, I AM!

I am Chad. I am the Pathfinder.

I believe that on the journey of becoming yourself, your life experiences mold you into the person you are today, but at the same time they lead you on a path back to who you were born to be. If we are brave enough and courageous enough to face our fears together, we will rise as the amazing, unique, gifted superhuman beings that we were created to be.

I send you blessings and wishes on your amazing journey in this life.

I love you. I hear you. I see you. I believe in you.

Much love.

Your brother,

Chad

"Here I Am"

I've been a star since I came out the womb
Came out my mama like a KING out his tomb
Resurrected, born into poverty
The intersections of my life tried to swallow me, follow me

Here I AM, on my own
I will not fall, I will not fail
I will prevail until the devil is gone

Here I AM, all alone
I once was blind but now I see
My DESTINY is what made me STRONG
HERE I AM

- Chad Diamond Dann

Questions on Your Path

IF YOU OBEY ALL THE RULES, YOU'LL MISS ALL THE FUN.

- Katharine Hepburn

1.

How can I follow my heart and uplift others?

2.

If I followed my intuition in every decision I made, what would my life be like?

3.

In this moment, am I inspired?

Transformation Affirmations

TRANSFORMATION ISN'T SWEET AND BRIGHT. IT'S
A DARK AND MURKY, PAINFUL PUSHING.
AN UNRAVELING OF THE UNTRUTHS YOU'VE
CARRIED IN YOUR BODY. A PRACTICE IN FACING
YOUR OWN CREATED DEMONS. A COMPLETE
UPROOTING, BEFORE BECOMING.

- Victoria Erickson

I created these affirmations to wake up in the morning feeling like a boss, to dance my way through the day, and to go to bed at night and sleep like a KING. My wish for you is that these affirmations will help you feel the same way. I love you so much for taking the time to make it this far. Carry on, Pathfinder!

For best results, say out loud and chant these affirmations as many times as you can in a row. Scream them at the top of your lungs, say them loud and proud with the people you love. Dance around, have fun. Feel the affirmations flowing through your entire body as you release them out into the universe!

1.

I RELEASE FEAR FROM EVERY CELL AND MY DNA

2.

THERE IS NO BLUEPRINT FOR AUTHENTICITY
I AM THE BLUEPRINT

3.

GOOD MORNING TO GREATNESS

LOVE YOURSELF

BE YOURSELF

FREE YOURSELF

Acknowledgments

Thank you to everyone
that I have ever crossed paths with in this life.
One way or the other, it made an impact on the
man I am today.

To all my brothers that have stood by my side,
I love you and see the greatness in you all.

To all my sisters that have stood by my side,
I love you and see the power in you all.

To the love of my life and my wife, Nealy Dann,
thank you for growing through this insanely crazy, beautiful,
messy as shit, extraordinary life with me.

ABOUT THE AUTHOR

C HAD DIAMOND DANN is a multi-passionate Award-Winning Documentary Filmmaker who believes we live in a world of unlimited possibilities. Chad is the owner of Grindstone Films, a video production company that specializes in showcasing individuals out there who are making an impact in their communities and the world.

Chad is currently manifesting his own traveling TV show where he explores the great mysteries of life. He is also creating new content for his YouTube channel showcasing all his talents.

He lives in Vancouver, WA, with his wife, Nealy, and their two cats, Tenzyn and Bella.

Check out his YouTube page at youtube.com/chaddiamonddann